WOMEN IN STEM
MARIE CURIE
RADIATION PIONEER

by Clara MacCarald

Ideas for Parents and Teachers

Pogo Books let children practice reading informational text while introducing them to nonfiction features such as headings, labels, sidebars, maps, and diagrams, as well as a table of contents, glossary, and index.

Carefully leveled text with a strong photo match offers early fluent readers the support they need to succeed.

Before Reading

- "Walk" through the book and point out the various nonfiction features. Ask the student what purpose each feature serves.
- Look at the glossary together. Read and discuss the words.

Read the Book

- Have the child read the book independently.
- Invite him or her to list questions that arise from reading.

After Reading

- Discuss the child's questions. Talk about how he or she might find answers to those questions.
- Prompt the child to think more. Ask: Did you know about Marie Curie and her discoveries before reading this book? What more would you like to learn about her life and work?

Pogo Books are published by Jump!
5357 Penn Avenue South
Minneapolis, MN 55419
www.jumplibrary.com

Library of Congress Cataloging-in-Publication Data

Names: MacCarald, Clara, 1979- author.
Title: Marie Curie: radiation pioneer / by Clara MacCarald.
Description: Minneapolis, MN: Jump!, Inc., [2024]
Series: Women in STEM | Includes index.
Audience: Ages 7-10
Identifiers: LCCN 2023024666 (print)
LCCN 2023024667 (ebook)
ISBN 9798889967071 (hardcover)
ISBN 9798889967088 (paperback)
ISBN 9798889967095 (ebook)
Subjects: LCSH: Curie, Marie, 1867-1934–Juvenile literature. | Women physicists–France–Biography–Juvenile literature. | Physicists–France–Biography–Juvenile literature. | Women chemists–France–Biography–Juvenile literature. | Chemists–France–Biography–Juvenile literature. | Poland–Biography–Juvenile literature.
Classification: LCC QD22.C8 M245 2024 (print)
LCC QD22.C8 (ebook)
DDC 540/.92 [B] –dc23/eng/20230525
LC record available at https://lccn.loc.gov/2023024666
LC ebook record available at https://lccn.loc.gov/2023024667

Editor: Katie Chanez
Designer: Emma Almgren-Bersie

Photo Credits: World History Archive/Alamy, cover (foreground); Shutterstock, cover (background), cover (X-ray); IanDagnall Computing/Alamy, 1, 4; New Africa/Shutterstock, 3; Lebrecht Music & Arts/Alamy, 5; Catarina Belova/Shutterstock, 6-7; Everett Collection Historical/Alamy, 8-9; Mushakesa/Shutterstock, 10; Chronicle/Alamy, 11; Xray Computer/Shutterstock, 12-13; Photo 12/Alamy, 14-15; Bettmann/Getty, 16-17; Drone Motion Stock/Shutterstock, 18; Pollyana Ventura/iStock, 19; gorodenkoff/iStock, 20-21; cunaplus/Shutterstock, 23.

Printed in the United States of America at Corporate Graphics in North Mankato, Minnesota.

TABLE OF CONTENTS

CHAPTER 1

EARLY LIFE

Marie Curie was a scientist. She lived at a time when it was hard for a woman to become one. But she did not let anyone stop her. She studied **radiation**. Her work changed the world.

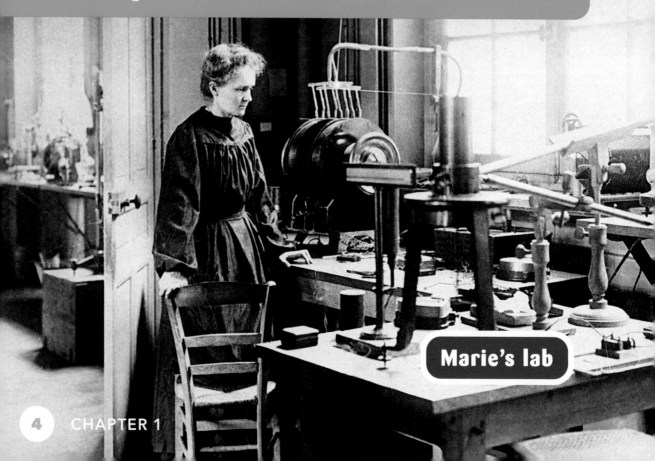

Marie's lab

Marie was born in Poland in 1867. She was the youngest of five children. Her parents were teachers. Marie loved learning. She was the top student in her class.

Marie

Marie wanted to study at a **university**. But her family didn't have much money. Marie needed to get a job. She worked as a **governess**.

By 1891, Marie earned enough money. But Polish universities did not let women in. So Marie went to France. There, she went to a university called Sorbonne. She studied **physics**.

DID YOU KNOW?

Marie gave one of her sisters money to study. Her sister became a doctor.

Sorbonne University

Pierre
Curie

While at school, she met another student. His name was Pierre Curie. They fell in love. They married in 1895.

CHAPTER 2

RADIOACTIVE DISCOVERIES

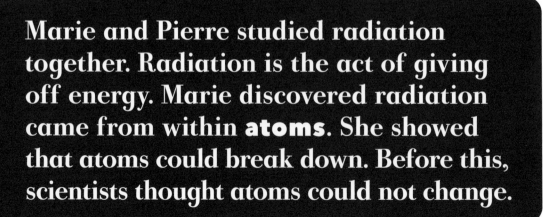

atom

Marie and Pierre studied radiation together. Radiation is the act of giving off energy. Marie discovered radiation came from within **atoms**. She showed that atoms could break down. Before this, scientists thought atoms could not change.

Heat is one kind of radiation. The kind of radiation the Curies studied is even more powerful. Very strong radiation can hurt people. The Curies believed radiation could also help people.

One way is with **X-rays**. Some machines use X-ray radiation to take pictures. The pictures show things inside a body. Doctors can see bones. Dentists can check teeth.

How does X-ray radiation work? Take a look!

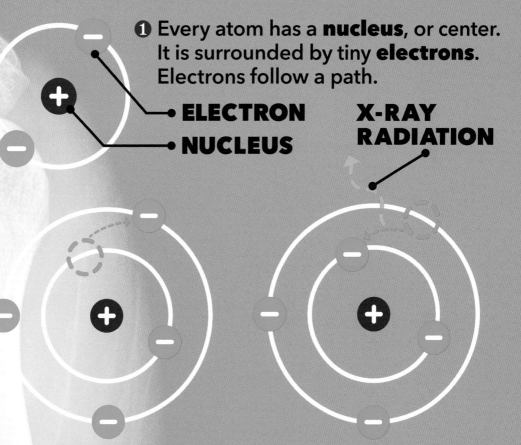

❶ Every atom has a **nucleus,** or center. It is surrounded by tiny **electrons**. Electrons follow a path.

ELECTRON

NUCLEUS

X-RAY RADIATION

❷ Electrons move between paths when given energy.

❸ The electrons go back to their original path. This movement releases energy. This energy is X-ray radiation.

In 1903, the Curies received a **Nobel Prize** for their work. Marie was the first woman to ever win one.

In 1906, Pierre died. Marie continued their work. She became a **professor** at Sorbonne. She was the first female professor in France.

DID YOU KNOW?

The Curies discovered two new **elements**. They were radium and polonium.

Marie teaching

Marie with U.S. President
Warren G. Harding

Marie continued to study radiation. She won a second Nobel Prize in 1911. She was the first person to win two.

Marie also traveled. She spoke to many people around the world. She wrote books. She wanted to spread knowledge about radiation.

DID YOU KNOW?

Marie came up with the word "**radioactive**." The Curies started using this new word in 1898.

CHAPTER 3

RADIATION TODAY

Marie died in 1934. But we see her work every day. **Nuclear power** plants are one place. They use radioactive matter to make energy.

nuclear power plant

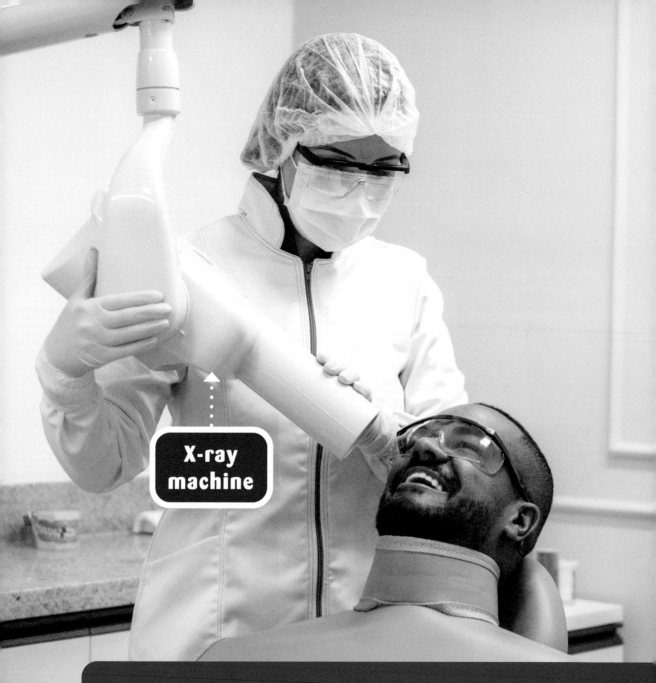

X-ray machine

Doctors and dentists use X-ray machines. Other types of radiation can help treat **cancer**. It kills cancer cells.

Many women saw what Marie did. It showed them what they could do. They decided to become scientists, too. What do you want to be when you grow up?

DID YOU KNOW?

Marie's daughter Irène became a scientist. Irène also won a Nobel Prize. She discovered how to make new radioactive elements.

ACTIVITIES & TOOLS

LOOKING INSIDE

Doctors use X-rays to see inside your body. But they can be dangerous without the right protection. Light is another kind of radiation. It is much safer than X-rays. See how X-rays work with this activity!

What You Need:
- paper
- pencil
- flashlight

1. Draw something, such as a bone, on a piece of paper.

2. Cover your drawing with a second sheet of paper. If you can see the pencil marks, add another sheet.

3. Hold the sheets of paper close to the light. Do you see your drawing?

An X-ray passes through skin, but not through things like bones. A similar thing happens with your light. The light passes through the paper. But light does not pass through the pencil lines. The pencil marks create a shadow you can see.

atoms: The smallest bits of pure matter.

cancer: A serious illness in which cells grow too fast and can destroy normal, healthy cells.

electrons: Tiny particles that move around the nucleus of an atom and have a negative charge.

elements: Substances that cannot be broken down into simpler substances.

governess: A person who often lives with a family and helps care for and teach the children.

Nobel Prize: A special award given to someone who does important things for the world.

nuclear power: A form of energy made by splitting atoms.

nucleus: The positively-charged central part of an atom that is made up of protons and neutrons.

physics: The study of energy and matter.

professor: A teacher in the highest teaching position at a university.

radiation: The act of giving off energy.

radioactive: Able to give off radiation.

university: A place where people study for degrees beyond high school.

X-rays: A type of radiation that is often used to look inside a person's body.

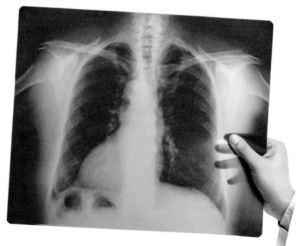

INDEX

TO LEARN MORE

Finding more information is as easy as 1, 2, 3.

1. Go to www.factsurfer.com
2. Enter "MarieCurie" into the search box.
3. Choose your book to see a list of websites.

FACT SURFER